Fiona Robertson is a specialist criminal barrister at 2 Hare Court. She is ranked as a leading junior in the Legal 500, is ranked in Chambers and Partners and was appointed junior Treasury Counsel in 2024.

Fiona is a highly sought after practitioner and is widely regarded as having a particular expertise in cases involving sexual offences, vulnerable witnesses and youths. Through this experience she developed an interest in the developing law in these areas and is also a contributing author to Rook and Ward on Sexual Offences: Law and Practise.

Fiona was called to the bar of England and Wales in 2008 and the bar of the Cayman Islands in 2012.

A Practical Guide to Applications Under Section 41 of the Youth Justice and Criminal Evidence Act 1999

A Practical Guide to Applications Under Section 41 of the Youth Justice and Criminal Evidence Act 1999

Fiona Robertson

Law Brief Publishing

Published 2024 by Law Brief Publishing, an imprint of Law Brief Publishing Ltd
30 The Parks
Minehead
Somerset
TA24 8BT

www.lawbriefpublishing.com

Paperback: 978-1-916698-47-5

For my daughter – a baby so relaxed she allowed me to pursue this project during maternity leave as well as welcoming her to the world

PREFACE

Despite s.41 being in force for almost 25 years it remains an area where practitioners struggle with the interpretation of the law and the adoption of the correct procedures in a timeous fashion. Too often applications are made late and fail to properly address the relevance of the evidence to the issues in the case while the interplay between section 41 and bad character evidence presents particular challenges. This can result in trials being delayed or, in extreme cases, trials being aborted altogether and the jury discharged with the ramifications as to costs and the impact on defendants and complainants that this brings. Section 41 is an issue that often burdens the appeal courts and there is now a plethora of case law as to the correct approach and scope of the provisions.

This book aims to break down the principles of section 41, by reference to the Youth Justice and Criminal Evidence Act 1999, the Criminal Procedure Rules and the interpretation of each from key case law. It is not intended to provide my views or comments on section 41, nor to be an exposition of the history of s.41 and every case arising in relation to it. Rather, I hope this book is of practical assistance to hard working, time pressed practitioners by providing a nutshell guide for use in the preparation of, and during, trials involving s.41 applications.

I have specialised in cases involving sexual offences for a number of years. This area has been of interest to me since studying law at university and I want to thank Professor Clare McGlynn who taught me many years ago at Durham University for igniting my interest in how the law impacts, protects and, at times, fails women. She has written extensively on topics including section 41, pornography, sexual violence and reforming rape laws and for commentary on such topics I cannot recommend anyone more highly.

The stated law is believed to be correct and up to date as at 1st August 2024.

Fiona Robertson
August 2024

CONTENTS

CHAPTER ONE

AN INTRODUCTION TO SECTION 41

The last hundred years have witnessed extensive developments in women's rights from suffrage, the sexual revolution of the 1960s and ultimately the legalisation of contraception and abortion. As attitudes have changed, so too has the law recognised the need for modernisation – criminalising rape within marriage and recognising men can also be victims of rape.

The law concerning the use of sexual behaviour evidence in trials has also developed with these changing attitudes, recognising that simply because a complainant consents to sexual intercourse on a previous occasion it does not follow that they were more likely to have consented to sexual intercourse on the occasion in question. It is, however, one thing for the law to recognise these essential facts but another for the law to put its principles into practise[1] and efforts to cease the humiliation of complainants in sexual offence trials with extensive, unnecessary and irrelevant questioning on their sexual behaviour have been slow but gradual.

Public concern over the conduct of cases involving sexual offences led to the Heilbron Report (1975) (Cmnd 6352) which considered and proposed reforms for rape trials. The Heilbron Report treated previous sexual association between the complainant and the accused as potentially relevant but advised that in general the previous sexual

---

1 Per Lord Hope of Craighead in *R v A (No. 2)* [2002] 1 AC 45

history of the complainant with other men was irrelevant and ought not to be introduced.

Following the Heilbron Report, section 2 of the Sexual Offences (Amendment) Act 1976 was enacted to restrict evidence or cross examination of a complainant's sexual experience with a person other than the accused. This was a restriction, rather than a prohibition, with section 2(2) providing that the judge shall give leave "if and only if he is satisfied that it would be unfair to that defendant to refuse to allow the evidence to be adduced or the question to be asked."

The Act did not, however, address cross examination or evidence of a complainant's sexual experience with the accused despite the concerns raised in the Heilbron Report. This failure, coupled with the broad discretion afforded to the trial judge, did not prevent the continued barrage of previous sexual behaviour evidence being adduced in trials, often with the aim of undermining a complainant's credibility.

The obvious risk of such evidence, and the use which a jury may make of it, was encapsulated by the 'twin myths' dicta in the Canadian case of *R v Seaboyer* [1991] 2 SCR 577:

> *"myths that unchaste women were more likely to consent to sexual intercourse and, in any event, were less worthy of belief. These twin myths are now discredited. The fact that a woman has had intercourse on other occasions does not in itself increase the logical probability that she consented to intercourse with the accused. Nor does it make her a liar."*

Recognising the fallacy of the 'twin myths', Lord Steyn, in *R v A (no 2)* [2002] 1 A.C. 45, observed that:

> *"such generalised, stereotyped and unfounded prejudices ought to have no place in our legal system. But even in the very recent past such defensive strategies were habitually employed.*

> *It resulted in an absurdly low conviction rate in rape cases. It also inflicted unacceptable humiliation on complainants in rape cases."*

The need for reform may have taken a further 23 years but more extensive restrictions on the use of evidence or questions about a complainant's sexual history were finally introduced by section 41 of the Youth Justice and Criminal Evidence Act 1999 which came into force on the 27th July 1999. Section 41 replaced the discretionary regime under s.2 of the Sexual Offences (Amendment) Act 1976 with a general exclusionary rule subject to leave of the trial judge and satisfying a restrictive set of exceptions. The restrictions aimed to debunk the 'twin myths' by balancing the need to protect complainants from humiliating, demeaning lines of cross examination with the defendant's right to a fair trial. Crucially, s.41 treats a complainant's sexual experience with the defendant the same as with other men but fairness is the underlying touchstone; a defendant should not be deprived of the opportunity to put relevant questions if exclusion of such questions could endanger the fairness of the trial.

Section 41 was considered extensively in *R v A (no 2)* [2002] 1 A.C. 45 with unanimous views expressed as to the need for restrictions on questioning and evidence regarding sexual behaviour of complainants. Lord Hope observed:

> *"the placing of restrictions on evidence or questions about the sexual behaviour of complainants in proceedings for sexual offences serves a legitimate aim. The prevalence of sexual offences, especially those involving rape, which are not reported to the prosecuting authorities indicates a marked reluctance on the part of complainants to submit to the process of giving evidence at any trial. The rule of law requires that those who commit criminal acts should be brought to justice. Its enforcement is impaired if the system which the law*

> *provides for bringing such cases to trial does not protect the essential witnesses from unnecessary humiliation or distress.....The law fails in its purpose if those who commit sexual offences are not brought to trial because the protection which is provided against unnecessary distress and humiliation of witnesses is inadequate. So too if evidence or questions are permitted at trial which lie so close to the margin between what is relevant and permissible and what is irrelevant and impermissible as to risk deflecting juries from the true issues in the case. The high rate of acquittals in rape cases before s.41 was introduced suggests that juries are not immune from temptation, and that they are quite likely to draw inference from evidence about a complainant's sexual behaviour on occasions other than that of the alleged rape which the law now recognises they should not draw."*

Similarly, Lord Hutton described there being three principal objectives of the law where the offence charged was rape – that a defendant should not be convicted of the crime with which he is charged when he has not committed it; that a defendant who is guilty of the crime with which he is charged should be convicted; and to ensure that a woman who complains she has been raped is treated with dignity in court and given protection against cross examination which invades her privacy unnecessarily and which subjects her to humiliating questioning and accusations which are irrelevant to the charge against the defendant. He recognised that evidence of the sexual history of the complainant had the potential to distort the course of the trial and divert the jury from the triable issue.

The question certified by the Court of Appeal which gave leave to appeal to the House of Lords in *R v A (No. 2)* and its detailed consideration was: "May a sexual relationship between a defendant and complainant be relevant to the issue of consent so as to render its exclusion under section 41 of the Youth Justice and Criminal

Evidence Act 1999 a contravention of the defendant's right to a fair trial?" In giving judgment Lord Steyn observed:

> *"as a matter of common sense, a prior sexual relationship between the complainant and the accused may, depending on the circumstances, be relevant to the issue of consent. It is a species of prospectant evidence which may throw light on the complainant's state of mind. It cannot, of course, prove that she consented on the occasion in question. Relevance and sufficiency of proof are different things."*

The interpretative obligation on Courts under s.3(1) of the Human Rights Act 1998 requires Courts, where possible, to read primary legislation in a way which is compatible with Convention rights. The Court concluded that section 41 must be read as permitting the admission of evidence or questioning which relates to a relevant issue in the case and which the trial judge considers is necessary to make the trial a fair one. This, therefore, lessened some of the constrictions on adducing sexual behaviour evidence without returning to the breadth of the former regime under s.2.

So has the introduction of s.41 had the desired effect of increasing conviction rates and restricting the use of sexual behaviour evidence in trials involving sexual offences? Convictions in rape trials remain woefully low consistently sitting around the 7% mark and so in this respect s.41 has had limited impact. However, while public perception may be that applications under s.41 are still being made and granted too frequently the statistics do suggest s.41 is achieving its aim of reducing the use of sexual behaviour evidence in trials and practitioners are heeding the warnings from established case law that s.41 applications involving sexual behaviour with a third party will rarely be relevant. In December 2017 the Ministry of Justice published a paper titled "Limiting the use of Complainants' Sexual History in Sex Cases" which examined the frequency and outcome of applications under section 41 through an analysis of 309 rape cases finalised in 2016. The paper found that s.41 applications were made in 40 cases (13%) of which the applications were granted in whole, or in part, by the court in 25 cases (8%). It is, therefore, clear no evidence pertaining to a complainant's sexual history was admitted in the vast majority of cases (92%). Of note 14 of the applications were opposed in their entirety by the prosecution (35%) while in 12 cases (30%) the prosecution did not oppose all, or part, of the s.41 application.

An independent review into s.41 commissioned by the Criminal Bar Association in October 2017 following the judgment in *R v Evans* [2016] EWCA Crim 452 surveyed responses from 140 practising criminal barristers. There was widespread consensus that restrictions on previous sexual behaviour evidence were warranted to eliminate questioning based on harmful stereotypes and myths but none of the respondents felt s.41 should be reformed to make it more restrictive. As ever the gap between the law and public perception raised concern, with many respondents observing that the public's lack of understanding of section 41 and how it applies, coupled with misreporting in the media of high-profile cases, could deter complainants from coming forward. It appeared the overlap and interplay between when a section 41 application should be made as against when a bad character application should be made presented real challenges for both practitioners and judges – a matter which is considered in detail in chapter 8.

What was plain from the review, however, was that section 41 applications were not being made lightly: with some applications being considered but not made and those that were being made were carefully scrutinised by prosecutors and judges. This is reflected in the statistics that show section 41 applications are not being made or granted as a matter of routine as some may fear.

Section 41 represents just one aspect of efforts by law makers to ensure the justice system does not re-traumatise or lose the faith of complainants in sexual offences. Improvements to police attitudes to complainants of sexual offences, the use of special measures including pre-recorded cross examination and reducing the time between reporting and trial also have a key role to play in encouraging complainants to come forward and securing convictions.

CHAPTER TWO

WHEN DOES SECTION 41 APPLY AND WHAT IS 'SEXUAL BEHAVIOUR'?

The procedures and time limits for making a section 41 application are governed by section 43 of the YJCEA 1999 and Part 22 of the Criminal Procedure Rules 2020 which are considered in detail in chapter 9.

Section 41 applies to trials involving sexual offences in both the Crown Court and Magistrates Court. In addition, as section 42(3) makes clear, it also applies to applications to dismiss, Newton hearings and the hearing of appeals. The references in section 41 to a person "charged with a sexual offence", therefore, include a person convicted of such an offence who falls to have a trial of issue prior to sentence or to appeal his conviction.

Section 41 goes considerably wider than s.2 of the Sexual Offences (Amendment) Act 1976 which applied to "rape offences". Section 41 applies to a "sexual offence" which includes any offence under Part 1 of the Sexual Offences Act 2003, or any relevant superseded offence, and human trafficking under s.2 of the Modern Slavery Act 2015 where committed with a view to sexual exploitation. This is an important extension to ensure vulnerable women trafficked to the UK to work in brothels are not subjected to intrusive, unfair cross examination on their work in the sex industry.

Section 41 restricts the admission of evidence or cross examination by or on behalf of any accused at the trial, about any sexual behaviour of the complainant. It does not, therefore, apply to the prosecution seeking to adduce such evidence – on occasion, for example, the prosecution may seek to adduce evidence of the complainant's virginity or sexual orientation as evidence to explain why they may not have consented to sexual activity with the defendant.

For the purposes of s.41, "sexual behaviour" is defined in s.42(1)(c) YJCEA 1999 as:

> *"any sexual behaviour or other sexual experience, whether or not involving any accused or other person, but excluding (except in section 41(3)(c)(i) and (5)(a)) anything alleged to have taken place as part of the event which is the subject matter of the charge against the accused".*

This definition, therefore, excludes any sexual behaviour between the defendant and complainant taking place immediately before the matter of the charge such as foreplay.

The definition of "sexual behaviour" in s.41(1)(c) is extremely wide and there will inevitably be borderline, fact specific, cases where it is a matter of impression and common sense as to whether the behaviour is sexual[2]. The complainant's perception of whether behaviour is 'sexual' is not determinative – such an approach would result in many vulnerable people, including children and those with learning difficulties, losing the protection of section 41 (*R v Etches* [2004] EWCA Crim 1313).

The phrase "sexual behaviour" is not limited to sexual experiences with the defendant or a third party nor is it limited to consensual, voluntary sexual behaviour as considered further in chapter 8. Although the definition obviously refers to conduct or activity of a sexual nature it

---

2 Per Sir Edwin Jowitt in *Mukadi* [2003] EWCA Crim 3765

can include verbal, rather than physical, exchanges and activities which need not necessarily involve any other person.

Sexual behaviour potentially includes:

a) Sexual activity with the defendant

b) Sexual activity with a person other than the defendant (*R v Mokrecovas* [2001] EWCA Crim 1644);

c) Social media posts or messages containing provocative posing or sexually charged messages (*R v D* [2011] EWCA Crim 2305; *R v Ben-Rajab and Baccar* [2012] 1 Cr App R4);

d) Completion of sexually explicit quizzes on the internet (*R v Ben-Rajab and Baccar* [2012] 1 Cr App R4);

e) Sexual orientation and identity (*R v Beedall* [2007] EWCA Crim 23; *R v T* [2021] EWCA Crim 318); and

f) Viewing pornography (*R v Ben-Rajab and Baccar* [2012] 1 Cr App R4).

As technology advances, so too must the law, in order to recognise the different ways people communicate. Certain mobile phone applications, websites and the manner in which individuals post content on social media may now come within "sexual behaviour". Whether such evidence, however, is relevant or admissible (rather than being adduced to try and impugn a complainant's credibility) will remain a further barrier particularly given the "complex mixture of motives which impels people, especially young people, to post messages on such sites".[3]

[3] Per Mackay J in *R v D* [2011] EWCA Crim 2305

The provisions of s.41 do not limit the meaning of "evidence" and, therefore, secondary evidence of sexual behaviour, for example having an abortion, may fall within s.41 as such evidence inferentially imports evidence of previous sexual activity. However, in *P (R)* [2014] 1 Cr App R 28 (401), the Court of Appeal concluded that although an abortion cannot result unless there has been sexual behaviour, questions about the fact of an abortion, and whether a defendant provided emotional succour and financial support for the complainant during the abortion procedure, did not make such questions "about" any sexual behaviour any more than, for example, questions about whether a mother was assisted by a defendant during a pregnancy were about sexual behaviour. In *P (R)* the Court concluded, however, that the questions were relevant as they detracted from the complainant's account that she viewed the defendant with distaste because of his sexual abuse of her but did not fall within s.41. This may be contrasted with the position in *R v PK* [2008] EWCA Crim 434 in which the Court of Appeal concluded the trial Judge was right not to permit cross examination on whether the defendant had taken the complainant to a clinic to get an abortion as the complainant had already accepted in cross examination that she had seen the defendant after the alleged abuse had ended and felt "fine" around him. The Court did not rule on whether s.41 could apply but concluded the evidence was likely to cause considerable distress for the complainant and only had very limited relevance in light of the evidence already given of post-abuse contact between the parties. It follows, therefore, that the basis and extent of questioning on such matters will be relevant in considering whether the proposed line of questioning is "about" sexual behaviour so as to fall within s.41 and whether it is admissible at all.

CHAPTER THREE

GATEWAY 1: A RELEVANT ISSUE OTHER THAN CONSENT

The first 'gateway' to admissibility is provided by section 41(3)(a) YJCEA 1999 where the evidence or question relates to a relevant issue in the case and that issue is not an issue of consent. A "relevant issue in the case" means any issue falling to be proved by the prosecution or defence in the trial of the accused (s.42(1)(a))

In *R v A (no 2)* [2002] 1 A.C 45, Lord Hope referred to evidence which is proffered for specific reasons pointing to guilt or innocence as opposed to impermissible generalisations about consent. He gave four examples of issues falling within "issue other than consent" as follows:

a) The defence of honest belief in consent – this is now likely to be of limited application as belief in consent has narrowed from an honest belief to a reasonable belief under the Sexual Offences Act 2003. Furthermore, such an issue is usually indivisible from the issue of consent.

   The Court of Appeal have firmly kept the gate shut on efforts to admit sexual history evidence under s.41(3)(a) where the motive of the evidence sought to be adduced appears, in reality, to be an attempt to engage one of the 'twin myths' by suggesting that because the complainant had sexual intercourse with someone else, they were more likely to have had consensual intercourse with the accused (eg *Harrison*

[2006] EWCA Crim 1543 and *Winter* [2008] EWCA Crim 8). In *R v Gjoni* [2014] EWCA Crim 691 the Court of Appeal concluded the trial judge was right to refuse the admission of evidence as to a conversation shortly before the alleged rape between the appellant and a third party that the complainant had previously engaged in sexual intercourse with the third party with the consent of her boyfriend and she may have sexual intercourse with them both that evening. The Court accepted the evidence could fall within s.41(3)(a) as the conversation went to the issue of why, on the evening of the alleged rape, the appellant had enquired of the complainant as to whether she would have sex with him – a suggestion which had angered her and she had rebuffed. The Court considered that the fact the third party had told the appellant he had previously had sexual intercourse with the complainant could not have amounted to any justification for a belief held by the appellant that the complainant would also consent to sexual intercourse with him when she had explicitly rejected him that very evening: the line of reasoning required – that a woman who consents to sexual intercourse with one comparative stranger will, a week later, consent to intercourse with another – was exactly that prohibited by s.41(4).

b) The complainant had motive to make up the allegation or was biased against the accused – where the jury has a range of possible explanations as to why a complainant may not be telling the truth about an allegation that do not involve sexual behaviour it may be unnecessary for a further basis to be evidenced through s.41 for the purposes of a fair trial (*R v DB* [2012] EWCA Crim 1235) as the defence case on any motivation to fabricate the allegation can be explored without reference to the complainant's sexual behaviour. Furthermore, where previous sexual behaviour evidence is relied upon for its relevance to a complainant's alleged motive to fabricate a complaint there needs to be a proper evidential basis for such an assertion. Where a defendant denies that any sexual activity took place, the previous sexual history of the complainant plainly has no bearing on it and so does not relate to the issue of consent under s.41(3)(a)). In *R v T* [2012] EWCA Crim 2358 the defendant denied that he had had sexual intercourse with the complainant. The question for the judge was whether a provocative photograph allegedly sent to the defendant by the complainant went to a relevant issue in the case. The Court of Appeal concluded it did go to a relevant issue since it was an issue falling to be proved by the defence in the trial of the accused, namely, that the motive for the complainant's false allegation was that she had been upset by the defendant's lack of interest in her.

A clear example of where previous sexual behaviour was inextricably linked to a motivation to fabricate allegations was in *R v F* [2005] 2 Cr App R 13. The complainant alleged her stepfather had systematically sexually abused her from the age of 7 to 16. The defendant denied any such sexual activity had taken place and asserted the allegation was fabricated out of revenge after he ended their consensual sexual relationship which had taken place when the complainant was aged 18 to 24. The prosecution case was that the complainant had been groomed – the defence, in contrast, asserted she was a willing and enthusiastic equal partner in the relationship. The Court of Appeal concluded photographs and videotapes of a pornographic nature made during the course of the adult relationship were relevant and admissible not only to the appellant's contention that the complaint of childhood abuse was motivated by a desire for revenge, but also to the jury's consideration of the even more critical question of whether the appellant had abused the complainant when she was a child. As the evidence related to a relevant issue in the case, the criteria for admissibility were established, and the evidence was not caught by s.41(4), the trial judge had no discretion to exclude it or limit its admission despite the graphic nature of the material the defence sought to be adduced.

c) There is an alternative explanation for the physical conditions on which the Crown relies to establish that intercourse took place – evidence, for example, of sexual activity with a third party might explain why the complainant fell pregnant, contracted a sexually transmitted infection or sustained injuries to the vagina or anus other than due to the defendant's alleged actions. In *R v L* [2015] EWCA Crim 741, the defendant's conviction for rape was quashed in light of fresh evidence indicating the complainant had been sexually abused (and may, on one interpretation, have been raped) as a 5 year-old. The complainant had asserted she was a virgin prior to being sexually abused by the defendant. The medical evidence indicated the complainant's hymen was disrupted in three places but this damage could not be attributed to one incident of rape rather than the other. The Court concluded that the evidence would have been admissible under s.41(3)(a) on the basis it provided an alternative explanation for damage to the complainant's hymen relied upon by the prosecution, other than rape by the defendant. Given the history of sexual violence against the complainant in this case, coupled with the fact the hymen may be damaged by non-penile penetration, it is perhaps surprising the prosecution sought to rely on such evidence as supportive of their case.

d) Details of the complainant's account must have come from other sexual activity before or after the event which provides an explanation for knowledge of that activity. This may apply, for example, in cases involving child sexual abuse where the

> prosecution argues that the complainant would not be able to describe the sexual activity if they had not experienced it with the defendant. It should, however, be recognised that with the development of structured sex education classes at school from a relatively young age, as well as the proliferation of depictions of sexual activity in television programmes, even young children may acquire knowledge of sexual practices from a variety of sources. (*R v MF* [2005] EWCA Crim 3376)

Added to these categories is the unusual, extremely fact specific, state of affairs that arose in *R v Ellis* [2005] EWCA Crim 3222. The appellant was charged with three counts of sexual intercourse with a woman who was suffering from a mental disorder, contrary to s.7(1) of the Sexual Offences Act 1956. He accepted having had a sexual relationship with his neighbour who suffered from a genetic chromosomal disorder but asserted he did not know and had no reason to suspect that she was suffering from a mental disorder as opposed to simply not very bright – consent was not, therefore, in issue. In quashing the conviction the Court of Appeal concluded that the trial Judge had erred in refusing an application under s.41 to adduce evidence that the complainant had a sex toy in her bedroom, watched pornographic movies and told the appellant she had engaged in sexual relations with others. These matters were relevant to how the appellant perceived the complainant's general conduct and social functioning as a counterbalance to the prosecution evidence that she acted like a child of 7 or 8 despite physically being an adult. If evidence that the complainant behaved like a child was relevant then so too was evidence as to the complainant's sexual behaviour which the jury should have been able to take into account in assessing what it was reasonable for the appellant to perceive as both an objective and subjective matter in relation to the complainant's mental state.

CHAPTER FOUR

GATEWAY 2: CONSENT AND CONTEMPORANEITY

Section 41(3)(b) applies where: the evidence or question relates to a relevant issue in the case; it is an issue of consent; and the sexual behaviour of the complainant to which the evidence or question relates is alleged to have taken place at or about the same time as the event which is the subject matter of the charge against the accused.

This gateway is typically used where there has been a pre-existing or ongoing consensual sexual relationship between the parties or where the complainant has made sexual advances towards others "at or about the same time" as the incident complained of. In *R v A (no. 2)* [2002] 1 A.C 45 Lord Steyn observed:

> *"as a matter of common sense, a prior sexual relationship between the complainant and the accused may, depending on the circumstances, be relevant to the issue of consent. It is a species of prospectant evidence which may throw light on the complainant's state of mind......It is true that each decision to engage in sexual activity is always made afresh. On the other hand, the mind does not usually blot out all memories. What one has been engaged on in the past may influence what choice one makes on a future occasion. Accordingly, a prior relationship between a complainant and an accused may sometimes be relevant to what decision was made on a particular occasion."*

Professor Clare McGlynn has countered this, however, by observing that:

> *"while it is commonly assumed that evidence of previous consensual sexual history is relevant to support an inference of consent, this approach must be challenged. While it might be possible to say, in some circumstances, that evidence of previous consensual relations is legally relevant, it being marginally more likely that sex was consensual than not, as a general proposition, this fails to take into account the variety of conditions within which sexual relations take place"*

Which may, for example, include abusive, coercive or controlling relationships. She observes that:

> *"assuming that someone is more likely to consent to sexual activity if they have done so in the past, is not so far away from the once-held assumption, and legal position, of implied consent during marriage."*[4]

Where the parties were married or in a relationship at the time of the alleged offence there is an obvious risk that the jury are likely to infer that there had been voluntary sexual intercourse previously and the events complained of must also have been consensual. In such circumstances the trial judge should direct the jury that they should draw no adverse inference because, under s.41, previous acts of voluntary sexual intercourse, without more, can have no bearing on any relevant issue in the case (*R v White* [2004] EWCA Crim 946).

---

4 McGlynn, C. (2017). Rape Trials and Sexual History Evidence: reforming the law on third party evidence. Journal of Criminal Law, 81(5) at 370

The statute does not provide any clarity as to what the vague phrase in s.41(3)(b) "at or about the same time" means. There is, therefore, no precise time limit for what constitutes "at or about the same time" but the courts have tended to adopt a restrictive approach. In *R v A (no. 2)* [2002] 1 A.C 45, Lord Slynn favoured a narrow interpretation which would not allow evidence of sexual behaviour to be adduced other than in cases where the acts relied on were *"really contemporaneous"*. Lord Steyn similarly acknowledged that the temporal restriction was *"extraordinarily narrow"* but nonetheless did not require extension to days, weeks or months. Lord Hope agreed that in the facts before the court the last act of consensual sexual intercourse was alleged to have taken place about a week before the alleged rape and did not, therefore, fall within the meaning of "at or about the same time" so as to be admissible.

Even if the behaviour satisfies the temporal requirement of s.41(3)(b) it does not necessarily follow that it will be relevant, relate to an issue of consent or that the judge will be satisfied that a refusal might render the jury's verdict unsafe. In *R v S* [2010] EWCA Crim 1579, for example, the Court of Appeal concluded that where it was perfectly clear to the jury that there was consensual sexual activity within an unhappy relationship prior to the alleged rape, the date of the last act of sexual intercourse (in this case the day before the offence) was not admissible as there was no logical connection between the last act of consensual intercourse and the event of the alleged rape.

CHAPTER FIVE

GATEWAY 3: CONSENT AND SIMILARITY

Section 41(3)(c) provides a gateway for admissibility where the evidence or question:

(a) relates to a relevant issue in the case;

(b) it is an issue of consent; and

(c) the sexual behaviour of the complainant to which the evidence or question relates is alleged to have been, in any respect, so similar

(i) to any sexual behaviour of the complainant which (according to evidence adduced or to be adduced by or on behalf of the accused) took place as part of the event which is the subject matter of the charge against the accused, or

(ii) to any other sexual behaviour of the complainant which (according to such evidence) took place at or about the same time as that event,

that the similarity cannot reasonably be explained as a coincidence.

This gateway applies not only to sexual activity with the accused but also to third parties. There is no temporal constraint (*R v T* [2004]

EWCA Crim 1220) and it can cover sexual behaviour occurring after, as well as before, the allegation charged, provided there is a sufficient chronological nexus between the events to render the previous behaviour probative (*R v G* [2016] EWCA Crim 1633; *R v Evans* [2016] EWCA Crim 452).

The need for some chronological nexus to qualify the sexual behaviour as occurring *"at or about the same time"* as the allegation was significant in *R v Gabbai* [2019] EWCA Crim 2287. The appellant and complainant, who were complete strangers, met in an Uber Pool taxi. They exited the taxi together and the complainant alleged that once she entered the appellant's property he immediately became very violent and raped her. The appellant sought to adduce evidence of the complainant's multiple previous allegations of rape and sexual assault under s.41(3)(a) on the basis it was not an issue of consent but was relevant to the appellant's reasonable belief in consent. The Court found the issue of consent and the appellant's reasonable belief in consent were indistinguishable in this case but concluded the evidence was of behaviour "highly similar" to that alleged in the appellant's case so as to fall within s.41(3)(c). The Court noted:

> *"although there was no suggestion of 'rough sex' or role play in the earlier episodes described by the complainant, that is not to exclude similarity 'in any respect' as the sub-section phrases it. The relevant similarities here are the admitted background of a chance meeting between strangers leading to an immediate sexual encounter, and to behaviour in the course of which the complainant…did not say no."*

The Court concluded, however, that the previous sexual behaviour neither took place as "part of the event which is the subject matter of the charge against" the appellant (s.41(3)(c)(i)) nor took place "at or about the same time of the event" (s.41(3)(c)(ii)) that was the subject of the charge. Therefore, although the Court considered the evidence was of real materiality it could not be admitted under s.41(3)(c) (the Court ultimately admitted it under s.100 CJA 2003 as there was an evidential basis to suggest the previous allegations were false).

The Court of Appeal have repeatedly described s.41(3)(c) as being a "high threshold" (*R v Guthrie* [2016] EWCA Crim 1633) and although on the face of it s.41(3)(c) is a narrow gateway there is no need for a "striking similarity" between the previous and current alleged conduct (as required for similar fact evidence per *DPP v Boardman* [1975] AC 421). What is instead required is a relevant similarity necessitating an exploration of circumstances, so as to avoid unfairness to the defendant. Lord Clyde in *R v A (No 2)* provided some guidance stating:

> *"It is only a similarity that is required, not an identity. .... Further the similarity must be such as cannot reasonably be explained as a coincidence. To my mind that does not necessitate that the similarity has to be in some rare or bizarre conduct. So long as the particular factor goes beyond the realm of what could reasonably be explained as a coincidence, it should suffice. Something about the sexual behaviour of the complainant on each of the occasions, such as something said or done by him or her which is not so unremarkable as to be reasonably explained as a coincidence has to be found."*

In *R v A (No 2)* the Court emphasised that the interpretative obligation on Courts under s.3(1) of the Human Rights Act 1998 which requires Courts, where possible, to read primary legislation in a way which is compatible with Convention rights. The Court concluded that section 41(3)(c) if read literally was *"disproportionately restrictive"* and must, therefore, be read as permitting the admission of evidence or questioning which relates to a relevant issue in the case and which the trial judge considers is necessary to make the trial a fair one. Lord Clyde observed:

> *"The context and the purpose of the evidence is not so much to show from past events that history has been repeated, as to indicate a state of mind on the part of the complainant towards the defendant which is potentially highly relevant to her state of mind on the occasion in question."*

This reading down of s.41(3)(c), therefore, has lessened some of the constrictions on adducing sexual behaviour evidence without returning to the breadth of the former regime under s.2 of the Sexual Offences (Amendment) Act 1976.

What will amount to evidence being "so similar" such that it cannot reasonably be explained as a coincidence will depend upon the facts of the case and inevitably, therefore, will vary from case to case. Although a "striking similarity" is not required it remains in practical terms a relatively high threshold – sexual identity or a particular form of sexual contact, without more, would not be sufficient as non-coincidental factors to meet s.41(3)(c). In *R v Aidarus* [2018] 6 WLUK 533, for example, the Court of Appeal emphasised that the fact oral sex was involved on an occasion other than that alleged could not provide the necessary degree of similarity. Indeed the application was described as having "*tested to the very limit the very rationale for enacting section 41 in the first place.*"

Even multiple factors of similarity may not be enough to bring the evidence within s.41(3)(c). In *R v Hamadi* [2007] EWCA Crim 3048 the Appellant sought to adduce previous sexual behaviour evidence with a third party which had similarities to the alleged offence namely: the complainant herself had instigated sexual activity; the activities took place outside in relatively public places; the activities took place in winter; and they took place when the complainant was in a relationship. The Court of Appeal rejected the argument concluding that the similarities could reasonably be explained as a coincidence, nor was the evidence truly probative in relation to the issue of consent.

Perhaps the most high profile s.41(3)(c) case, due to the public outcry it caused at the time, is that of *R v Evans* [2016] EWCA Crim 452 in which the Court of Appeal allowed an appeal against conviction by a Welsh footballer convicted of rape after new evidence emerged from two witnesses who had sex with the complainant in similar circumstances to the appellant. The complainant had no memory of the alleged rape, her evidence being that she had been extremely drunk the night before and did not remember what had happened. The appellant had asserted in interview that the complainant had been having sexual intercourse with his friend and he was invited to join in by both parties. He disclosed she had adopted a position on all fours and directed him to penetrate her harder. Following his convictions two witnesses came forward to report having had sexual intercourse with the complainant during which she had positioned herself on all fours and demanded they "go harder" – the appellant sought to adduce this evidence under s.41(3)(c).

The court observed that when the appellant was first asked by police what happened,

> *"he had described in graphic detail the sexual behaviour of a woman who, on the prosecution case, would have been incapable of behaving in that way. If the jury rejected his account of her sexual behaviour, he had no defence. Two other men have described specific instances of her behaving in a very similar fashion with them, in the days before the alleged rape and in the days that followed. On each occasion she had been drinking, she is said to have instigated certain sexual activity, directed her sexual partner into certain positions, and used specific words of encouragement."*

The Respondent sought to argue that there was nothing 'unusual' about the complainant's alleged behaviour. The Court rejected this argument emphasising *"the behaviour does not have to be unusual or bizarre; it has to be sufficiently similar that it cannot be explained reasonably as a coincidence."* The Court considered on the facts of the case, the evidence of the two third parties would have been relevant and admissible evidence at trial and was arguably sufficiently similar to come within the terms of s.41(3)(c) (and potentially s.41(3)(a) on the issue of reasonable belief.)

Dame Vera Baird KC, the former Solicitor General and Victims' Commissioner for England and Wales, expressed concern that the Court of Appeal in *Evans* had lowered the bar of admissibility for evidence of complainants' sexual history and the judgment represented a return to the mindset and practices that had been confined to history. She noted that to avoid losing the recent upturn in rape reporting the courts must be vigilant and protect women from being unfairly judged on their sexual history. A number of academics also expressed concern that the admission of evidence relating to the complainant's sexual past – which in the *Evans* case included evidence of casual sex and excessive drinking – creates a challenge to a complainant's 'moral credibility' with the result that juries consider complainants to be less credible thereby rendering acquittals more likely.[5]

While such concerns were entirely understandable at the time, it is apparent since that *Evans* has been treated as a case very much turning on its facts and does not appear to have opened the floodgates to applications under s.41(3)(c) as initially feared. The risks of indirect challenges to a complainant's 'moral credibility' through the

---

5 McGlynn, C. (2018). Challenging the law on sexual history evidence: a response to Dent and Paul. Criminal law review, 2018(3) at 221; Aileen McColgan, 'Common Law and the Relevance of Sexual History Evidence' (1996) 16 Oxford Journal of Legal Studies 275; Michele Burman, 'Evidencing sexual assault: women in the witness box' (2009) 56 Probation Journal 379

admission of sexual history evidence, however, remain and judges must be careful to address such inappropriate judgments through legal directions on rape myths which now form a standard part of summing up in cases involving sexual offences.

CHAPTER SIX

GATEWAY 4: REBUTTAL AND EXPLANATION

In addition to the three gateways in section 41(3) the YJCEA 1999 provides a fourth gateway through section 41(5) YJCEA 1999 – the 'rebuttal' or 'explanation' gateway. Section 41(5) arises if the evidence or question:

(a) relates to any evidence adduced by the prosecution about any sexual behaviour of the complainant; and

(b) in the opinion of the court, would go no further than is necessary to enable the evidence adduced by the prosecution to be rebutted or explained by or on behalf of the accused.

Both limbs must be satisfied for an application under s.41(5) to succeed. The necessity for rebuttal does not, however, allow a 'free for all' approach to sexual behaviour evidence and the evidence to be adduced must address the specific evidence to be rebutted. In *R v Steltner* [2018] EWCA Crim 1479 the Court of Appeal concluded the trial Judge was right to refuse an application to adduce evidence that the complainant had previously been digitally penetrated in response to her assertion that she was a virgin, noting there was a clear distinction between both acts. As *Steltner* demonstrates, the prosecution may adduce evidence of a complainant's lack of sexual experience or her attitudes towards sexual activity in order to bolster or explain why the complainant did not consent to the offence in question. Rebuttal evidence may be adduced under s.41(5) where there is evidence to the contrary provided it specifically addresses and rebuts the prosecution evidence.

Section 41(5) will not, however, apply in cases where a statement made by a complainant as to her sexual behaviour is not relied upon by the prosecution or not relied upon for the truth of its contents. In *R v Gulab Singh* [2003] EWCA Crim 485, for example, the prosecution did not seek to rely on the complainant's assertion that she was a virgin as part of their case – evidence of sexual intercourse between the complainant and a third party was not, therefore, admissible under s.41(5). In contrast, in *R v Aidarus* [2018] EWCA Crim 2073 and *R v Soroya* [2006] EWCA Crim 1884 false statements by complainants as to a lack of sexual experience in an effort to avoid being raped were relied upon by the prosecution – not for the truth of their contents, but rather for the fact of what was said at the relevant time. In *Soroya* the Court of Appeal rejected an argument that s.41 should apply to the prosecution as the prohibitions otherwise operate in an unbalanced, unfair manner against the defendant. The Court of Appeal noted that s.78 of the Police and Criminal Evidence Act 1984 could be deployed where s.41 might otherwise produce an adverse effect upon the fairness of the proceedings.

Two matters obviously flow from the existence of the section 41(5) gateway. First, the prosecution must disclose to the defence any material capable of rebutting evidence about the sexual behaviour of the complainant which they intend to adduce – such material would plainly be capable of undermining the prosecution case or assisting the defence. Second, the restriction on admissibility under section 41(4) – namely that no evidence or question shall be regarded as relating to a relevant issue in the case if it appears to the court to be reasonable to assume that the purpose (or main purpose) for which it would be adduced or asked is to establish or elicit material for impugning the credibility of the complainant as a witness – does not apply to evidence to be adduced under s.41(5).

In *R v F* [2005] 2 Cr App R 13, considered previously in chapter 3, the prosecution relied on evidence from the complainant as to the adult relationship between the parties and the nature of it. The Court of Appeal noted that the dispute about the nature of the adult relationship between the parties — submission, or happy participation—was vital to the jury's decision as to whether there had indeed been an earlier abusive relationship yet the video and photographic evidence, which was of potential value to the resolution of the dispute, was not before the jury. Without the video and photographic evidence the jury may well have concluded that the relationship was indeed one in which the complainant simply submitted to the appellant as the appellant was deprived of the evidence which may have supported his assertions that she was a happy and enthusiastic participant in the adult sexual relationship. The Court concluded the evidence should, therefore, have been admitted under s.41(5).

The phrase 'evidence adduced by the prosecution' in section 41(5)(a) covers evidence of prosecution witnesses and evidence of other witnesses under cross-examination by the prosecution. In *R v Hamadi* [2007] EWCA Crim 3048, in order to ensure a fair trial, the Court of Appeal favoured a wide reading of s.41(5) to also cover something said by a prosecution witness in cross examination provided the evidence is not deliberately elicited by defence counsel and was potentially damaging to the defence case. The Court, however, considered that even on a liberal reading of s.41(5), evidence from the complainant that she would not have had sexual relations with anyone other than her boyfriend which was elicited after defence counsel had pursued a specific line of questioning could not properly be considered evidence adduced by the prosecution rather than by the defence.

It is debatable whether a liberal reading of s.41(5) has, in fact, been adopted by the Court of Appeal. In *Hamadi* it was accepted the line of questioning was not designed to deliberately adduce the complainant's evidence that she would not have had sexual relations with anyone other than her boyfriend. The Court nonetheless concluded the evidence that she had previously had sexual relations with a third party was not admissible under s.41(5). While such evidence does at first blush appear relevant to the complainant's credibility, the Court of Appeal has made clear that a complainant's statement about being in a close, loving relationship is not necessarily false merely because she also has a sexual relationship with another man and such questions inevitably fall within the meaning of 'sexual behaviour' in section 41 (*Winter* [2008] EWCA Crim 3; *Hamadi* [2007] EWCA Crim 3048).

The rebuttal gateway is inevitably fact specific and less commonly employed than other gateways as a means of admissibility. Examples from case law include: where a complainant asserted she was a virgin but had previously attended a sexual health clinic for a pregnancy test (*R v JD McG* [2001] EWCA Crim 1976); and evidence that a complainant had previously attributed her pregnancy to someone else and been prescribed oral contraceptives where she had alleged she was not sexually active with anyone else and the defendant was responsible for her pregnancy (*F* [2008] EWCA Crim 2859). These examples plainly went to, but no further than, to rebut the evidence adduced by the prosecution from the complainants in the respective cases.

The evidence must, however, be relevant to, and capable of explaining or rebutting, the matter led by the prosecution rather than simply seeking to adduce previous sexual conduct to suggest the complainant must have consented on the occasion in question. In *R v Costanzo and Orlando* [2021] EWCA Crim 615 the overall thrust of the complainant's evidence was that she could not remember what had happened but that she did not believe that she would have consented to a threesome in a nightclub with two strangers or have given that impression, because she had never done that before. The Court of Appeal, in rejecting the appeal against conviction concluded:

"If there was any evidence to the contrary, then section 41(5) might well bite. That would be evidence and there would be a proper basis for questioning necessary to enable X's evidence to be rebutted or explained on behalf of the applicants. But there was no such evidence or basis. The fact that X did or may have had any number of sexual liaisons with different men (who were known to her and one at a time) in completely different circumstances over the preceding days was neither here nor there. Cross-examination about those matters would not rebut or explain the assertion being made by X. Rather, it would offend the objection to one of the twin myths, namely that a woman's previous sexual conduct sheds light on whether she consented on the occasion being litigated."

CHAPTER SEVEN

RESTRICTIONS ON ADMISSIBILITY

Section 41 provides a number of checks and balances such that even where one of the gateways is met, there are further grounds on which an application may be refused. Section 41(2) makes clear that the Court may not give leave in relation to any evidence or question regarding the sexual behaviour of the complainant unless it is satisfied not only that one of the gateways in s.41(3) or s.41(5) apply but also "that a refusal of leave might have the result of rendering unsafe a conclusion of the jury or (as the case may be) the court on any relevant issue in the case".

In *R v T* [2021] EWCA Crim 318 the defendant appealed against his conviction on the basis he was wrongly precluded from asking the complainant, his former wife whom he was accused of raping, questions relating to her sexual orientation, including whether she had been conflicted about her sexual identity and had made the allegations as a means of justifying any change in her sexual identity. The Court of Appeal determined that the purpose of the questioning was speculative and designed to impugn the credibility of the complainant. The application could not, therefore, meet the requirements of s.41(2)(b). The Court considered this was:

> *"a paradigm case of questions being sought to be asked which would have needlessly humiliated and invaded the privacy of a complainant. Giving evidence at a rape trial is stressful enough. To have had to answer questions in public about her sexuality and her alleged internal conflicts about her sexuality would only have added to the mortification and distress of the*

> *complainant (as the appellant must have appreciated). Accordingly, even if, contrary to our own view, section 41 had no application here then, in any event, this line of questioning was properly to be excluded: in effect for the reasons given by the judge herself. It was speculative and irrelevant and of no probative value. Consequently, on ordinary evidential principles it was rightly not put before the jury."*

This need to satisfy both limbs of s.41(2), therefore, restricts the admission of evidence on sexual behaviour to cases where it is truly relevant and probative to the issue the jury must determine.

Section 41(6) provides a further restriction requiring that the evidence or question relates to a specific instance or instances of sexual behaviour on the part of the complainant. This, therefore, expressly prohibits evidence about general reputation or generalised sexual behaviour – in *R v T* [2021] EWCA Crim 318 for example, the Court of Appeal concluded questioning the complainant about her sexual identity amounted to questioning about sexual behaviour but was wholly generalised and thus fell to be excluded by section 41(6) as well as s.41(2)(b).

Section 41(6) is also likely to restrict evidence as to reputation including the complainant's past and ongoing activities as a prostitute – the Court of Appeal have considered otherwise such an argument is:

> *"tantamount to the proposition that any sexual encounter of a complainant will satisfy section 41(6) if it happens to be possible to assign a date and place to that conduct. If that were all the subsection meant it would amount to very little indeed. In our judgment, the subsection only possesses intellectual coherence if it is taken to require that there must be something about the circumstances of a specific episode of alleged sexual*

> *conduct by a complainant which has potential probative force"* (*R v White* [2004] EWCA Crim 946).

In *White* the Court rejected the notion that a wider reading for s.41 by force of s.3 of the Human Rights Act 1998 was required where the evidence concerned sexual acts between the complainant and third parties.

Once it is established that the criteria for admitting the evidence are established then, subject to s.41(4) the Court has no discretion to refuse to admit it. In *R v F* [2005] 2 Cr App R 13 the Court of Appeal noted:

> *"It is sometimes loosely suggested that the operation of s.41 involves the exercise of judicial discretion. In reality, the trial judge is making a judgment whether to admit, or refuse to admit evidence which is relevant, or asserted by the defence to be relevant. If the evidence is not relevant, on elementary principles, it is not admissible. If it is relevant, then subject to s.41(4) and assuming that the criteria for admitting the evidence are established, in our judgment the court lacks any discretion to refuse to admit it, or to limit relevant evidence which is properly admissible. In short, once the criteria for admissibility are established, all the evidence relevant to the issues may be adduced. As part of his control over the case, the judge is required to ensure that a complainant is not unnecessarily humiliated or cross-examined with inappropriate aggression, or treated otherwise than with proper courtesy. All that is elementary, but his obligation to see that the complainant's interests are protected throughout the trial process does not permit him, by way of a general discretion, to prevent the proper deployment of evidence which falls within the ambit permitted by the statue merely because, as here, it comes in a stark, uncompromising form"*

The restriction afforded by s.41(4) is, however, the most difficult hurdle to overcome and applies where the defence seek to adduce evidence or ask questions through the 41(3) gateways. Section 41(4) provides: "for the purposes of subsection (3) no evidence or question shall be regarded as relating to a relevant issue in the case if it appears to the court to be reasonable to assume that the purpose (or main purpose) for which it would be adduced or asked is to establish or elicit material for impugning the credibility of the complainant as a witness."

The term "credibility" in s.41(4) does not exclude evidence that undermines a complainant's account of the allegation at trial. Indeed, the Court of Appeal recognised in *R v V* [2016] EWCA Crim 1434, if that were the case, the subsection:

> "*would exclude almost all defence evidence or cross-examination, as the purpose of that is almost always to suggest that the complainant is wrong and the defendant is not guilty.*"

Rather, s.41(4) acts as a filter to prevent the introduction of evidence that generally suggests the complainant is the type of person whose word should not be believed through proper consideration of the motivation for the proposed line of questioning. This approach was emphasised by the Court of Appeal in *R v F* [2005] EWCA Crim 493; [2005] 2 Cr App R 13 when it recognised:

> *"in one sense, of course, any evidence which directly challenges the evidence of a complainant, or seeks to demonstrate a malicious motive, involves an attack on her credibility. However merely because cross-examination of the complainant may impugn her credibility....it does not necessarily follow that the purpose, or the main purpose for deploying it is to do so."*

This position was reiterated more recently in *R v Evans* [2016] EWCA Crim 452. The Respondent sought to interpret s.41 to mean that even if a judge ruled questions about the complainant's sexual conduct with two third parties to be admissible, the defence would be bound by her answers; they would be unable to call evidence about her sexual conduct because the evidence would go to her 'credit'. The Court of Appeal rejected this argument as betraying a misunderstanding of the section:

> *"If the proposed questioning of the witness or the evidence the defence wish to adduce goes solely or mainly to the issue of the credibility of the complainant, it would be prohibited by subsection (4); the judge would not give leave. We emphasise the words solely or mainly. To an extent any challenging of a complainant's evidence involves an attack upon her credibility. To obtain leave under this section the defence must satisfy the judge that the provisions of one or more of the other subsections apply and that, if leave is refused, any subsequent conviction would be unsafe. Thus, it is only if the proposed questioning and evidence of specific instances of sexual behaviour relate to a relevant issue and either do not go to the issue of consent under subsection (3)(a) or do go to the issue of consent and the requirements of subsection (3) (b), (c) (i) or (c) (ii) are fulfilled that a judge may give leave. If the judge gives leave the section makes clear provision for the asking of questions and the calling of evidence. The defence could not possibly be 'bound' by the complainant's answers."*

In *R v T* [2021] EWCA Crim 318 the Court of Appeal went further acknowledging that there may be situations where evidence about previous sexual behaviour can properly be admitted where relevant to the complainant's motive to fabricate evidence, even though it may also bring into play questions of credibility. The Court considered, however, it was necessary:

> *"to be wary about the potential for assertions to the effect that the challenge is as to malicious motivation to fabricate being, in truth, an obfuscation of the real or main purpose: that is to say, to undermine a complainant's credibility. Were it otherwise, then the provisions of section 41(3)(a) could be used to ride a coach and horses through the desirable policy reflected in section 41(4) of the 1999 Act".*

Such a judgement will inevitably be a determination for the trial judge weighing up the facts of the case as against the basis for the application.

CHAPTER EIGHT

PREVIOUS ALLEGATIONS

Perhaps one of the most significant, but difficult, areas in the law governing sexual offences is the interplay between s.41 of the Youth Justice and Criminal Evidence Act 1999 and s.100 of the Criminal Justice Act 2003 where a complainant has made a previous allegation of a sexual offence. Where a truthful allegation has previously been made such evidence is unlikely to be relevant or to meet the hurdles of s.41 (see, for example, *R v Pike* [2022] EWCA Crim 1501). Equally where an allegation is genuinely false such evidence is likely to be relevant and admissible as a means of challenging both the complainant's credibility and whether there had been a sexual assault at all (*Nagrecha* [1997] 2 Cr App R 401). In such cases, s.41 is not engaged as the evidence relates to untruthful conduct, not sexual behaviour, however the Court retains a discretion to exclude the evidence under s.78 PACE 1984 if the evidence is too speculative or prejudicial.

An example of where the defence may seek to rely on previous allegations without asserting that they are necessarily false may arise where the defence suggest the complainant has transposed abuse suffered by the complainant at the hands of another onto the defendant. In *R v BJK* [2024] EWCA Crim 667 the Court of Appeal considered such a line of questioning would engage s.41 and required a detailed consideration of what the complainant had alleged of the other males alleged to have abused her as regards physical acts, locations, identities and circumstances. This led to the conclusion that the scope for mistakenly attributing to the appellant abuse which the complainant had sustained at the hands of one of the others was:

> *"minimal to the point of being non-existent. There are a number of features which singly and cumulatively show that the suggestion of 'transposition' is without evidential foundation and purely speculative."*

The Court emphasised that s.41 was designed to prevent this type of speculative roaming through a complainant's sexual history. LJ Stuart-Smith observed that the complainant having to give evidence about the abuse perpetrated by the appellant was bad enough but:

> *"having to go into the sexual behaviour of others could only and would markedly increase the humiliation and harassment and is precisely what section 41 was designed to prevent."*

In *R v RT and MH [2001] EWCA Crim 1877*, which involved two interlocutory appeals, the Court of Appeal dealt with the correct construction of s.41 in cases involving previous allegations of sexual offences. The Court concluded that questions about false statements in the past by a complainant about sexual assaults or questions about a failure to complain about the alleged assault which is the subject matter of the charge while complaining about other sexual assaults are not questions "about" any sexual behaviour of the complainant. Such questions do not relate to the Complainant's sexual behaviour but to her statements in the past or her failure to complain and do not, therefore, fall within section 41. The Court observed there was nothing to suggest that the purpose of section 41 was to exclude such evidence or questions, even if they are seen as going principally to credibility. This position was subsequently affirmed in *R v S* [2009] EWCA Crim 2457.

Although there will be cases at either end of the spectrum – some where a previous complaint is clearly untrue and the defence should obviously be permitted to cross examine on it, and others where there is overwhelming evidence a previous allegation is true – most cases are likely to fall between these two extremes. This may include, for example, the not uncommon scenario where previous allegations by a complainant have been retracted, not pursued or not charged. Where defendants seek to adduce evidence of such complaints in an effort to demonstrate the complainant has made a false allegation in the past and is not, therefore, a credible witness present particular challenges as to whether such an application should fall under s.41 YJCEA or s.100 CJA 2003.

In *R v AM* [2009] EWCA Crim 618 the Court of Appeal made clear that in order to avoid possible abuse, judges should not regard evidence or questions as being about a previous false complaint, (rather than about the complainant's sexual behaviour) unless there is a proper evidential basis for asserting that the previous complaint made was untrue.

Similarly, in *RT and MH* [2001] EWCA Crim 1877 Keene LJ observed:

> *"However, it is open to a judge to guard against abuse of the system. The defence, wishing to put questions about alleged previous false complaints, will need to seek a ruling from the judge that section 41 does not exclude them. It would be professionally improper for those representing the defendant to put such questions in order to elicit evidence about the complainant's past sexual behaviour as such under the guise of previous false complaints. But in any case the defence must have a proper evidential basis for asserting that any such previous statement was (a) made and (b) untrue. If those requirements were not met, then the questions would not be about lies but would be 'about the sexual behaviour of the complainant' within the meaning of section 41(1). The judge is entitled to seek assurances from the defence that it has a*

> *proper basis for asserting that the statement was made and was untrue."*

In *R v AM* the Court of Appeal recognised the difficulty lay in assessing what constituted a proper evidential basis. The Court of Appeal suggested:

> *"it is less than a strong factual foundation for concluding that the previous complaint was false. But there must be some material from which it could properly be concluded that the complaint was false."*

The Court considered that in applying this test judges would not be assisted by an examination of the facts of other cases as the exercise which a judge is called on to perform is fact sensitive. The assessment is not an exercise of discretion, but rather a judgement on the basis of all the relevant material.

An acquittal of the previous alleged offender, a decision not to charge or a reluctance on the part of the complainant to report matters will not necessarily be sufficient to meet the threshold of a proper evidential basis to conclude the previous complaint is false. As with directions to the jury in offences involving sexual offences the court must guard against rape myths when assessing evidence relating to previous complaints of sexual offences – there may, for example, be any number of reasons why a complainant made a late, reluctant or inconsistent complaint, or did not ultimately pursue a complaint, but this does not necessarily equate to the complaint being false. It is rare for applications to admit evidence of untested allegations to succeed due to the obvious risk of the trial descending into satellite litigation as to the truth or otherwise of previous complaints which will be impossible to establish within the confines of the trial before the jury.

It is not, however, necessary for the evidence to conclusively demonstrate that the previous complaint was false. Instead the Judge must conduct a fact specific analysis to assess if there is some material from which it could properly be concluded that the complaint was false (*R v AM* [2009] EWCA Crim 618) or whether there is a proper basis to allege the complaints were false (*R v Knight* [2013] EWCA Crim 2486). In *R v AM* the trial Judge had failed to ask himself the relevant question whether, on the material before him, depending on the answers given by the complainant, the jury could have been satisfied that the previous complaint was false. Had the judge done so he should have concluded that the jury could have been so satisfied in that case.

In *R v Abdelrahman* [2005] EWCA Crim 1367 the Court of Appeal concluded the trial judge had been right to refuse the appellant's application to adduce evidence of allegations of rape that may have previously been made by the complainant. The Court noted that the fact the allegations had not been taken to court was not the same as the allegations having been admitted to be, or found to be, false. On a proper analysis there was no proper evidential basis for asserting that the previous allegations were untrue. The questions, therefore, fell within s.41 and were not admissible by virtue of s.41(4) as the questions sought to impugn the credibility of the complainant.

This approach was adopted in *R v All-Hilly* [2014] 2 Cr App R 33 with the Court of Appeal ruling that the fact the complainant had made but did not pursue previous allegations did not provide a sound basis for suggesting they were false allegations so as to fall under s.100 CJA rather than s.41. Going further, the Court of Appeal has observed that a failure to co-operate may or may not justify a conclusion than an allegation is false depending on the circumstances (*R v V* [2006] EWCA Crim 1901). In *R v JD McG* [2001] EWCA Crim 1976, for example, new evidence arose following the appellant's conviction of a previous complaint of sexual misbehaviour by the complainant against a third party which had not been disclosed to the defence prior to trial. The evidence concerned either an allegation of rape, as a first complaint witness testified to, or, at least, an allegation of unlawful sexual intercourse, as the complainant disclosed. The defence asserted the allegations were untrue as demonstrated by the complainant's refusal to support the rape complaint when interviewed by the police and the fact there was no adverse response from her when the matter was not pursued. The Court of Appeal quashed the conviction, concluding the evidence would be admissible at trial and of a potentially significant nature.

In *R v Gabbai* [2019] EWCA Crim 2287, considered previously in chapter 5, the appellant's convictions for rape were overturned after the Court of Appeal concluded the complainant's multiple previous allegations of rape should have been admitted under s.100 CJA 2003. The appellant asserted that the material, comprised of GP notes and counselling records which detailed previous allegations of sexual assault and rape, were replete with inconsistencies and contradictions. It was asserted, therefore, that there was material on which the jury could conclude that the complaints were false. The records expressed the complainant's doubts as to whether the previous acts had been non-consensual and included what appeared to be self-descriptions that she was *"lying. Attention seeker."* The Court of Appeal concluded that the material was capable of giving rise to a number of inferences: first that the complainant placed herself in risky situations and engaged in sexual encounters with strangers; second that she often engaged in sex when she was at the least ambiguous as to consent but "did not say no"; third that she gave a history of rapes but had never pursued a complaint of rape; and fourth, that she, herself, doubted her own accounts of rape having commented to medical professionals *"maybe it wasn't rape"*. The third and fourth inferences bore directly on the complainant's credibility and the Court concluded the:

> *"evidence was of a striking nature, and relevant as suggestive of previous false accounts. The evidence that the complainant had doubted her own past suggestions of rape and was 'Lying. Attention seeker' should have been admitted pursuant to s.100 CJA 2003. This provided an evidential foundation for a conclusion of falsity, of substantial importance in the case as a whole, and should have been before the jury."*

Although evidence and challenge as to complaints and the falsity of them goes to a complainant's credibility such evidence can be led as part of the defence case if the complainant is not prepared to admit that she has previously lied about a relevant collateral matter (*R v JD McG* [2001] EWCA Crim 1976).

Where it can be established that a previous complaint was false so as to fall outside s.41 a non-defendant bad character application under s.100 CJA 2003 is still likely to be required and prosecutors should consider carefully the circumstances and context of any false complaint when deciding whether to oppose such an application given the importance of a complainant's credibility in cases of this nature.

In *R v T* [2014] EWCA Crim 618 the appellant had sought to introduce evidence from the complainant about alleged lies she had told about her previous sexual experience – it was asserted she would lie in order to get attention. The appellant argued the evidence was not evidence of prior sexual conduct because it was not relied upon as being truthful but rather as dishonest attention seeking – the complainant having accepted the school rumours of her previous sexual activity were untrue. On this basis s.41 was not engaged but s.100(1)(c) of the Criminal Justice Act 2003 was. The Court of Appeal observed it was:

> *"of the first importance to consider the context and to underline the age of C and her friends (one of whom*

demonstrated that she had no real understanding of what sexual intercourse was) and to exercise particular care when considering whether the evidence did, in fact, have substantial probative value. This is not a case of a false complaint about a sexual matter: there is no suggestion either in what C said to her friends or in the rumours that she was ever complaining about the activities of anyone else other than the appellant. Further, precisely what, if any, sexual experience that C might have had could never be an appropriate area of investigation (which is likely to have been the effect of permitting this line of cross examination bearing in mind the extremely generalised nature of the available evidence of lack of truthfulness)." On this basis the Court concluded the judge was entitled to reach the conclusion that this material should not be admitted.

CHAPTER NINE

PROCEDURE FOR MAKING A S.41 APPLICATION AND COUNSEL'S RESPONSIBILITIES

The procedures and time limits for making a section 41 application are governed by section 43 of the YJCEA 1999 and Part 22 of the Criminal Procedure Rules 2020. The key rules are as follows:

a) A defendant who wants to introduce evidence or cross-examine a witness about any sexual behaviour of the complainant must serve an application in writing on the court officer and each other party as soon as reasonably practicable after becoming aware of the grounds for doing so and, in any event, not more than 10 business days after the prosecution disclose material on which the application is based (CrimPR 22.4(1)). Thus, even where an issue arises during the course of a trial the application must be reduced to writing and not dealt with 'off the cuff'.

b) CrimPR 22.4(2) sets out that the application must:

   i. Identify the issue to which the defendant says the complainant's sexual behaviour is relevant.

   ii. Give particulars of any evidence that the defendant wants to introduce and any questions that the defendant wants to ask. This gives the court the ability to maintain control over the questioning (if the application is permitted) and prevents the defence from going into areas that would be forbidden by section 41 and/or outside the parameters established by the Judge's ruling.

iii. Identify the particular gateway(s) relied upon.

iv. Include the name and date of birth of any witness whose evidence about the complainant's sexual behaviour the defendant wants to introduce.

c) The prosecution have 10 business days to respond in writing to the defence application explaining the grounds for their objection (CrimPR 22.6).

d) An application can only be granted by a judge. The prosecution can opt not to oppose an application under s.41 but cannot consent to such an application.

e) The Criminal Procedure Rules permit the court to vary the timetable for the application and response even after the expiry of the time limits (CrimPR 22.8). This power is plainly necessary where applications arise unexpectedly during the course of a trial as a result of the evidence given. The judge's discretion to vary the timetable should not, however, be used by practitioners to excuse or circumvent the time limits and procedures set out within the Criminal Procedure Rules.

f) Applications must be heard in private and in the absence of the complainant (section 43(1) YJCEA 1999 and CrimPR22.2(1)). The Court must not determine the application unless each party other than the applicant is present or has had at least 10 business days in which to make representations and the court is satisfied that it is has been able to take adequate account of the complainant's rights (CrimPR 22.2(1)(b)).

g) The court must announce the reasons for either allowing or refusing the application and, if the application is allowed, the extent to which evidence may be introduced or questions asked (CrimPR 22.3(3)) at a hearing in public.

The prosecutor must inform the complainant of the court's decision as soon as reasonably practicable and explain any arrangements that, as a result, will be made for them to give evidence. The court must allow sufficient time for this to take place (s.43(2) and CrimPR 22.3).

In *Crossland* [2013] EWCA Crim 2313 the Court of Appeal emphasised that the rules on how a section 41 application should be made are there for a reason. Although a failure to comply with the proper procedure for such applications is not a basis to refuse an application it:

> *"makes it more likely that things will go wrong at the trial, either because the statutory protection given to the complainants in sexual offence proceedings will be undermined or because the defence will be prohibited from pursuing a legitimate line of questioning".*

In *Crossland* the breaches were *"serious and inexcusable"* meaning the basis for the application and the questions the defence wanted to ask were not clearly articulated to the trial judge.

For section 41 applications to be readily understood, and thus more likely to succeed, it is important that the defence statement identifies any issue which may be relevant to the application such as a hostile motive of the complainant. In *R v T* [2012] EWCA Crim 2358 the defence argued the Judge had erred in refusing to allow cross examination of the complainant on a provocative photograph and Facebook messages she had allegedly sent to the defendant. The application was made without notice, following the complainant's evidence in chief and was intended to show a hostile motive – an issue not raised in the defence statement. The Court of Appeal noted that the:

> *"ambush by the defence led, as so often it tends to do, to error. That is part of the danger which arises from an unjustifiable breach of the rules of advance disclosure".*

The Court noted it had been *"incumbent"* on the defence to give advance notice of the material sought to be adduced under s.41 so as to give the prosecution sufficient time to consider whether it might want to obtain evidence as to the source and credibility of the material. The Court concluded, however, that the photograph the defence sought to adduce did go to a relevant issue, namely, that the complainant was interested in the defendant and the motive for her false allegation was her affront at his lack of interest. Once that relevance had been established, the judge had no discretion to refuse to allow the matter to be put to the complainant or for the defendant to give evidence about it (*R v F* [2005] Cr App R 13). In particular, it was not open to the judge to refuse to allow the matters to be put because they had been raised so late in the day – the timing of the application did not affect the admissibility of the photograph but rather the weight to be attached to it and the question of whether the defendant had obtained the photograph by means other than it being sent by the complainant directly to him.

The Court further noted it was not open to the judge to refuse to allow the Facebook entries to be put merely on the basis that there had been no advance notice of the intention to adduce them in evidence. But the judge was entitled to refuse to allow the defence to do so in the form in which they were produced whereby the context of any response from the defendant was entirely lacking. Absent any evidence as to whether, and if so how, the appellant obtained the photograph; when he obtained it; why no advance notice of it was given in his defence statement or subsequently; and as to why no s.41 application was made earlier, it was not possible for the Court of Appeal to say whether the judge's failure to allow the photograph to be adduced afforded a ground for allowing the appeal. The appeal, therefore, had to be adjourned for a further hearing, at which both appellant and prosecution would have the opportunity to adduce any relevant evidence they wished to rely upon as to the provenance of the evidence and whether there was a reasonable explanation for the late emergence of this evidence at trial.

Although a breach of the rules does not, therefore, provide a basis to refuse a s.41 application, practitioners instructed in cases in which s.41 arises must be aware of the procedures and deadlines for making and opposing such applications. This requires a significant degree of early preparation and consideration of the likely trial issues before the stage 2 date.

Both prosecution and defence counsel should give consideration to the contents of the witness's statement or ABE interview where it raises potential s.41 issues. For example, where sexual history is mentioned, prosecutors should consider whether this is evidence that the prosecution would want to adduce or whether this evidence should be edited out from an ABE or not adduced from the witness in evidence in chief. If the information is not to be adduced the defence should be advised in writing or at the PTPH and appropriate edits proposed so all parties understand the parameters of the evidence to be given. If the defence object, they must then make a section 41 application.

The same position applies to comments made by a defendant in their police interview. Defendants may make comments which would be in contravention of the section 41 restrictions. Prosecutors should be alive to this possibility and seek to edit these comments out of an interview where appropriate.

At the Plea and Trial Preparation Hearing (PTPH), the defence should endorse the PTPH form indicating whether they intend to make a section 41 application and the court should be invited to set a timetable. The defence must give proper notice of any section 41 application and clearly identify the issue to which the defendant says the complainant's sexual behaviour is relevant – this should be linked to any matters subsequently raised in the defence statement so the relevance of the application can clearly be understood in the context of the issues in the case. The defence must also give particulars of any evidence that the defendant wants to introduce, the questions that the defendant wants to ask and the particular gateway(s) relied upon. If an application is served late, the defence must be prepared to have the reasons for any delay scrutinised at court.

When a section 41 application is received from the defence, best practise is for the prosecution reviewing lawyer to review the application, request written advice from counsel on the application, discuss the application and proposed response with counsel at a case conference and approve the response to the section 41 application prior to service.

If the defence serve a s.41 application late, the prosecution should enquire as to the reason the application is late and ask the court to scrutinise the reasons provided. Prosecutors should, however, recognise that there will be cases where there is a genuine reason for late service of a section 41 application – for example, it may have been prompted by a matter that has only recently come to the attention of either the prosecution or the defence – and whether any unfairness or prejudice in fact arises from late service.

Where the court has allowed the introduction of evidence or cross-examination about the complainant's sexual behaviour the prosecutor must inform the complainant as soon as reasonably practicable (Part 22.3(1)(a) CrimPR 2020).

Under s.17(4) YJCEA a complainant in respect of a sexual offence is eligible for special measures unless they decline such measures. Where a s.41 application is granted the status of special measures should be reconsidered – a complainant may feel more comfortable giving evidence with the benefit of special measures particularly if they know they are going to be asked questions about their sexual history. The prosecution has 10 business days following a section 41 application being granted to apply for a special measures direction or variation of an existing special measures direction (CrimPR part 22.7). The Court must also give directions for the appropriate treatment and questioning of the witness ("ground rules" for the conduct of questioning).

It is the responsibility of the prosecuting advocate to challenge cross examination which is irrelevant, inappropriate or which falls within the restrictions of s.41. Prosecuting advocates should be protective and proactive where there is a breach of section 41 and should not rely solely on judicial intervention to stop questioning or evidence being adduced in contravention of the s.41 restrictions.

In some cases, consideration may have to be given, where irrelevant and prejudicial evidence has been adduced without leave, to asking the court to discharge the jury. This is a drastic step, and the needs of the complainant will have to be balanced against the need to secure a fair trial for both the prosecution and defence. This illustrates the importance of understanding the section 41 provisions and ensuring that they are complied with.

APPENDIX A

COUNSEL'S RESPONSIBILITIES CHECKLIST

Defence:

- Endorse the PTPH form to address whether the defence intend to make a section 41 application.
- Give proper notice of any section 41 application
- Clearly identify the issue to which the defendant says the complainant's sexual behaviour is relevant cross referencing to details contained within the defence statement.
- Give particulars of any evidence that the defendant wants to introduce, the questions that the defendant wants to ask and the particular gateway(s) relied upon.
- Comply with the time limits set out in the CrimPR – if an application is served late, set out the reasons for the delay and be prepared to have such reasons scrutinised at court.

Prosecution:

- Consider the contents of the witness's statement or ABE interview. Where sexual history is mentioned, consider whether this is evidence that the prosecution would want to adduce or whether this evidence should be edited. If the information is not be adduced it must be edited, and the defence should be advised in writing or at the PTPH that this evidence is not relied upon.

- Consider the defendant's police interview and propose edits where appropriate if the defendant has made comments which would be in contravention of the section 41 restrictions. The defence must be informed and either agree such edits or make a s.41 application.

- When a section 41 application is received from the defence, the reviewing lawyer must:

  a) Review the application.

  b) Reach a preliminary position on how the Crown will respond.

  c) Respond to the application.

  d) Request written advice from counsel on the application.

  e) Discuss the application and proposed response with counsel at a case conference.

  f) Approve the response to the section 41 application prior to service.

- When an application has been granted by the court in advance of the trial date, the reviewing lawyer must:

    a) Inform the complainant of the court's decision as soon as is reasonably practicable.

    b) Reconsider special measures and, if appropriate, apply for a new special measures direction (CPR part 22.7) within 10 business days of a section 41 application being granted.

- At the PTPH, prosecutors should ensure that the defence endorse the PTPH form on whether they intend to make a section 41 application and invite the court to set a timetable for the application.

- If the defence serve an application late, the prosecution must enquire as to the basis for the late application and ask the court to scrutinise the reasons provided.

- Where the court has allowed the introduction of evidence or cross-examination about the complainant's sexual behaviour the prosecution must inform the complainant as soon as reasonably practicable (Part 22.3(1)(a) CPR 2020) even if the application is granted during the course of the trial.

- Be prepared to challenge inappropriate cross examination or irrelevant evidence which breaches any s.41 ruling.

APPENDIX B

41.— RESTRICTION ON EVIDENCE OR QUESTIONS ABOUT COMPLAINANT'S SEXUAL HISTORY

(1) If at a trial a person is charged with a sexual offence, then, except with the leave of the court—

(a) no evidence may be adduced, and

(b) no question may be asked in cross-examination,

by or on behalf of any accused at the trial, about any sexual behaviour of the complainant.

(2) The court may give leave in relation to any evidence or question only on an application made by or on behalf of an accused, and may not give such leave unless it is satisfied—

(a) that subsection (3) or (5) applies, and

(b) that a refusal of leave might have the result of rendering unsafe a conclusion of the jury or (as the case may be) the court on any relevant issue in the case.

(3) This subsection applies if the evidence or question relates to a relevant issue in the case and either—

(a) that issue is not an issue of consent; or

(b) it is an issue of consent and the sexual behaviour of the complainant to which the evidence or question relates is alleged to have taken place at or about the same time as the event which is the subject matter of the charge against the accused; or

(c) it is an issue of consent and the sexual behaviour of the complainant to which the evidence or question relates is alleged to have been, in any respect, so similar—

(i) to any sexual behaviour of the complainant which (according to evidence adduced or to be adduced by or on behalf of the accused) took place as part of the event which is the subject matter of the charge against the accused, or

(ii) to any other sexual behaviour of the complainant which (according to such evidence) took place at or about the same time as that event,

that the similarity cannot reasonably be explained as a coincidence.

(4) For the purposes of subsection (3) no evidence or question shall be regarded as relating to a relevant issue in the case if it appears to the court to be reasonable to assume that the purpose (or main purpose) for which it would be adduced or asked is to establish or elicit material for impugning the credibility of the complainant as a witness.

(5) This subsection applies if the evidence or question—

(a) relates to any evidence adduced by the prosecution about any sexual behaviour of the complainant; and

(b) in the opinion of the court, would go no further than is necessary to enable the evidence adduced by the prosecution to be rebutted or explained by or on behalf of the accused.

(6) For the purposes of subsections (3) and (5) the evidence or question must relate to a specific instance (or specific instances) of alleged sexual behaviour on the part of the complainant (and accordingly nothing in those subsections is capable of applying in relation to the evidence or question to the extent that it does not so relate).

(7) Where this section applies in relation to a trial by virtue of the fact that one or more of a number of persons charged in the proceedings is or are charged with a sexual offence—

(a) it shall cease to apply in relation to the trial if the prosecutor decides not to proceed with the case against that person or those persons in respect of that charge; but

(b) it shall not cease to do so in the event of that person or those persons pleading guilty to, or being convicted of, that charge.

(8) Nothing in this section authorises any evidence to be adduced or any question to be asked which cannot be adduced or asked apart from this section.

MORE BOOKS BY LAW BRIEF PUBLISHING

'A Practical Guide to Confiscation and Restraint' by Narita Bahra QC, John Carl Townsend, David Winch
'A Practical Guide to the Law of Forests in Scotland' by Philip Buchan
'A Practical Guide to Health and Medical Cases in Immigration Law' by Rebecca Chapman & Miranda Butler
'A Practical Guide to Bad Character Evidence for Criminal Practitioners by Aparna Rao
'A Practical Guide to Extradition Law post-Brexit' by Myles Grandison et al
'A Practical Guide to Hoarding and Mental Health for Housing Lawyers' by Rachel Coyle
'A Practical Guide to Psychiatric Claims in Personal Injury – 2nd Edition' by Liam Ryan
'Stephens on Contractual Indemnities' by Richard Stephens
'A Practical Guide to the EU Succession Regulation' by Richard Frimston
'A Practical Guide to Solicitor and Client Costs – 2nd Edition' by Robin Dunne
'Constructive Dismissal – Practice Pointers and Principles' by Benjimin Burgher
'A Practical Guide to Religion and Belief Discrimination Claims in the Workplace' by Kashif Ali
'A Practical Guide to the Law of Medical Treatment Decisions' by Ben Troke
'Fundamental Dishonesty and QOCS in Personal Injury Proceedings: Law and Practice' by Jake Rowley
'A Practical Guide to the Law in Relation to School Exclusions' by Charlotte Hadfield & Alice de Coverley
'A Practical Guide to Divorce for the Silver Separators' by Karin Walker
'The Right to be Forgotten – The Law and Practical Issues' by Melissa Stock
'A Practical Guide to Planning Law and Rights of Way in National Parks, the Broads and AONBs' by James Maurici QC, James Neill et al
'A Practical Guide to Election Law' by Tom Tabori
'A Practical Guide to the Law in Relation to Surrogacy' by Andrew Powell
'A Practical Guide to Claims Arising from Fatal Accidents – 2nd Edition' by James Patience
'A Practical Guide to the Ownership of Employee Inventions – From Entitlement to Compensation' by James Tumbridge & Ashley Roughton
'A Practical Guide to Asbestos Claims' by Jonathan Owen & Gareth McAloon

'A Practical Guide to Stamp Duty Land Tax in England and Northern Ireland' by Suzanne O'Hara
'A Practical Guide to the Law of Farming Partnerships' by Philip Whitcomb
'Covid-19, Homeworking and the Law – The Essential Guide to Employment and GDPR Issues' by Forbes Solicitors
'Covid-19 and Criminal Law – The Essential Guide' by Ramya Nagesh
'Covid-19 and Family Law in England and Wales – The Essential Guide' by Safda Mahmood
'A Practical Guide to the Law of Unlawful Eviction and Harassment – 2nd Edition' by Stephanie Lovegrove
'Covid-19, Brexit and the Law of Commercial Leases – The Essential Guide' by Mark Shelton
'A Practical Guide to Costs in Personal Injury Claims – 2nd Edition' by Matthew Hoe
'A Practical Guide to the General Data Protection Regulation (GDPR) – 2nd Edition' by Keith Markham
'Ellis on Credit Hire – Sixth Edition' by Aidan Ellis & Tim Kevan
'A Practical Guide to Working with Litigants in Person and McKenzie Friends in Family Cases' by Stuart Barlow
'Protecting Unregistered Brands: A Practical Guide to the Law of Passing Off' by Lorna Brazell
'A Practical Guide to Secondary Liability and Joint Enterprise Post-Jogee' by Joanne Cecil & James Mehigan
'A Practical Guide to the Pre-Action RTA Claims Protocol for Personal Injury Lawyers' by Antonia Ford
'A Practical Guide to Neighbour Disputes and the Law' by Alexander Walsh
'A Practical Guide to Forfeiture of Leases' by Mark Shelton
'A Practical Guide to Coercive Control for Legal Practitioners and Victims' by Rachel Horman
'A Practical Guide to the Law of Driverless Cars – Second Edition' by Alex Glassbrook, Emma Northey & Scarlett Milligan
'A Practical Guide to TOLATA Claims' by Greg Williams
'A Practical Guide to Elderly Law – 2nd Edition' by Justin Patten
'A Practical Guide to Responding to Housing Disrepair and Unfitness Claims' by Iain Wightwick

'A Practical Guide to the Law of Bullying and Harassment in the Workplace' by Philip Hyland
'How to Be a Freelance Solicitor: A Practical Guide to the SRA-Regulated Freelance Solicitor Model' by Paul Bennett
'A Practical Guide to Prison Injury Claims' by Malcolm Johnson
'A Practical Guide to the Small Claims Track – 2nd Edition' by Dominic Bright
'A Practical Guide to Advising Clients at the Police Station' by Colin Stephen McKeown-Beaumont
'A Practical Guide to Antisocial Behaviour Injunctions' by Iain Wightwick
'Practical Mediation: A Guide for Mediators, Advocates, Advisers, Lawyers, and Students in Civil, Commercial, Business, Property, Workplace, and Employment Cases' by Jonathan Dingle with John Sephton
'The Mini-Pupillage Workbook' by David Boyle
'A Practical Guide to Crofting Law' by Brian Inkster
'A Practical Guide to the Law of Domain Names and Cybersquatting' by Andrew Clemson
'A Practical Guide to the Law of Gender Pay Gap Reporting' by Harini Iyengar
'NHS Whistleblowing and the Law' by Joseph England
'Employment Law and the Gig Economy' by Nigel Mackay & Annie Powell
'A Practical Guide to Noise Induced Hearing Loss (NIHL) Claims' by Andrew Mckie, Ian Skeate, Gareth McAloon
'An Introduction to Beauty Negligence Claims – A Practical Guide for the Personal Injury Practitioner' by Greg Almond
'Intercompany Agreements for Transfer Pricing Compliance' by Paul Sutton
'Zen and the Art of Mediation' by Martin Plowman
'A Practical Guide to the SRA Principles, Individual and Law Firm Codes of Conduct 2019 – What Every Law Firm Needs to Know' by Paul Bennett
'A Practical Guide to Adoption for Family Lawyers' by Graham Pegg
'A Practical Guide to Industrial Disease Claims' by Andrew Mckie & Ian Skeate
'A Practical Guide to Conducting a Sheriff Court Proof' by Andrew Stevenson
'A Practical Guide to Vicarious Liability' by Mariel Irvine
'A Practical Guide to Applications for Landlord's Consent and Variation of Leases' by Mark Shelton
'A Practical Guide to Relief from Sanctions Post-Mitchell and Denton' by Peter Causton

'A Practical Guide to Equity Release for Advisors' by Paul Sams
'A Practical Guide to Financial Services Claims' by Chris Hegarty
'The Law of Houses in Multiple Occupation: A Practical Guide to HMO Proceedings' by Julian Hunt
'Occupiers, Highways and Defective Premises Claims: A Practical Guide Post-Jackson – 2nd Edition' by Andrew Mckie
'A Practical Guide to Financial Ombudsman Service Claims' by Adam Temple & Robert Scrivenor
'A Practical Guide to Running Housing Disrepair and Cavity Wall Claims: 2nd Edition' by Andrew Mckie & Ian Skeate
'A Practical Guide to Holiday Sickness Claims – 2nd Edition' by Andrew Mckie & Ian Skeate
'Arguments and Tactics for Personal Injury and Clinical Negligence Claims' by Dorian Williams
'A Practical Guide to Drone Law' by Rufus Ballaster, Andrew Firman, Eleanor Clot
'A Practical Guide to Compliance for Personal Injury Firms Working With Claims Management Companies' by Paul Bennett
'RTA Allegations of Fraud in a Post-Jackson Era: The Handbook – 2nd Edition' by Andrew Mckie
'RTA Personal Injury Claims: A Practical Guide Post-Jackson' by Andrew Mckie
'On Experts: CPR35 for Lawyers and Experts' by David Boyle
'An Introduction to Personal Injury Law' by David Boyle

www.ingramcontent.com/pod-product-compliance
Lightning Source LLC
LaVergne TN
LVHW022312200926
848481LV00004B/1305
* 9 7 8 1 9 1 6 6 9 8 4 7 5 *